SEASONAL LOVE

LOVE IS NOT UNCONDITIONAL

AF558860

RITESH MISHRA

Copyright © Ritesh Mishra
All Rights Reserved.

ISBN 979-888606100-0

This book has been published with all efforts taken to make the material error-free after the consent of the author. However, the author and the publisher do not assume and hereby disclaim any liability to any party for any loss, damage, or disruption caused by errors or omissions, whether such errors or omissions result from negligence, accident, or any other cause.

While every effort has been made to avoid any mistake or omission, this publication is being sold on the condition and understanding that neither the author nor the publishers or printers would be liable in any manner to any person by reason of any mistake or omission in this publication or for any action taken or omitted to be taken or advice rendered or accepted on the basis of this work. For any defect in printing or binding the publishers will be liable only to replace the defective copy by another copy of this work then available.

Firstly, my this book of poetry ***SEASONAL LOVE*** is specially dedicated to all who taught me the meaning of love either by their support, care and encouragement or by their natural reaction.

secondly, this book is also dedicated to all the true lover who gave their best in love and accepted his or her loved one whom they have loved more than their life but in return were left heartbroken.

Contents

About Poet *vii*

Preface *ix*

Acknowledgements *xi*

Prologue *xiii*

Journey Between Dream, Friendship And Love

1. Friend In Need Is A Friend Indeed 3
2. What Beauty Means To Me 4
3. What You Are For Me 5
4. My Love Life 6
5. Happy Women's Day 7

VALENTINE WEEK SPECIAL

6. Happy Rose Day 11
7. Happy Propose Day 12
8. Happy Chocolate Day 14
9. Happy Teddy Day 15
10. Happy Promise Day 16
11. Happy Hug Day 17
12. Happy Kiss Day 18
13. Happy Valentine Day 19

BIRTHDAY SPECIAL

14. Happy Birthday 23
15. Best Wishes To You 24
16. Happy Birthday Sweetheart 25
17. Happy Birthday My Love 26

Contents

BLEEDING HEART

18. With Broken Heart 31

19. Life Without You 33

20. How Can I Forget You 34

21. My Dear Love, I Miss You 36

Tips To Remain Happy 37

About Poet

RITESH MISHRA is a well-known name in Healthcare industry for his medical expertise and outstanding management skill. He is a quality consultant for healthcare organisation as well as a certified NABH Internal Auditor.

Also, He is an Editor of a well-known book "Medical Tourism in India (India - a new hub of medical tourism)" and Author of books like Conceptual Optometry (care for an eye); A textbook of basic optometry; Management of Hospital and the most recent is Corona Virus Disease (COVID-19). He has been awarded and honoured with Six sigma medical excellence award for high altitude medical service for 2014 & 2015.

He has attempted to try his hand in poetry which has been his passion from childhood. This is his first book of poetry that collects the poem from journey of love from dream, friendship, love to break up and life after that. Hope you will enjoy reading.

Contact at email: riteshmishra4k@gmail.com

Preface

Everyone want to be loved unconditionally. But unfortunately, love is not unconditional. One whoever get in touch with you and connect to you have some reason and motive. Here, We meet people and stay in relation for some period and love arise. The journey of love remain alive until there is mutual respect for each other or motive is not achieved.

This book of Poetry **SEASONAL LOVE** : ***Love is not unconditional*** is a collection of poems of dreams, love and care, heartbreaking and self control. Also, This book contain motivational quotes to bring some interesting connection of poem with love and reality.

Hope you will enjoy reading..

Acknowledgements

"The foundation stones for a balanced success are honesty, character, integrity, faith, love and loyalty."

There are many hands that joined together to protect me and stand as my strength in difficult conditions. I am thankful to them for their effort of tolerating me as long as they can.

Special thanks to all those person who taught me the real meaning of love. brining this book SEASONAL LOVE is possible because of the experience that I get and learn from life.

I tried my best to give a realistic image of love with this generation and current scenario of our society. Thank you all for your support and keep loving.

Acknowledgments

[illegible]

Prologue

This poetry book is composed of various poems that describe the journey of boy from dream, friendship to love and getting apart due to complicated circumstances.

The poetry refers to the experience of a boy in love and based on his experience how he wished his girlfriend on every special day of valentine weeks, women's day and made her feel special.

The boy described his love for her through the poetry in different section and due to some reasons, they separate their path and how the boy react to the breakup as bleeding heart in memory of his beloved is described perfectly.

He summarized his short duration love as ***Seasonal Love*** that begin with a dream, friendship followed by love relation but unfortunately come to an end without a happy ending.

Journey Between Dream, friendship and Love

1. Friend in need is a friend indeed

Friend is one who gives you hope when your morale is low,
Friend is a place when you feel alone where you can easily go.
Friend is those who never demand promises or expectation,
Friend is true when there is trust, sincerity and bond creation.
Friend is someone who makes your fun but believe in you,
Friend is only one who listen you carefully and your every view.
Friend is stars in night who overcome darkness with their light,
Friend is one who give right advice and makes your future bright.
Friend is one who respect differences and creates a silent bond.
Friend is what become closer as it grows older and makes it strong.
Friend is one who justify your garden self being blooming flower,
Friend is a person who is available for you at every hour.
Friend is the first relation in the earth which never dies,
Friend is relation of strong faithful bonding that god has ties.
Friend is ever there in tough time whenever you need,
Friend is so called friend in need is friend indeed.

2. What Beauty means to me

Beauty is not what your physical appearance expresses but it's what ur heart reflect,
Beauty is not what you dress but it's what your brain demonstrates,
Beauty is not what you make up but it's what u speak up,
Beauty is not what u spend but it's what u donate,
Beauty is not what attraction you pile but it's what you give others smile,
Beauty is not in your body but it's what your nature,
Beauty is not what you look but it's in what decision you took,
Beauty is reflection of your inner soul n connect other to appraise,
then see what reputation your inner beauty within you will raise.

3. What you are for me

A beauty entered in my life as rays of hope
Spread peace acting similar to religious tope
Chain of work she perform daily beats all lope
Encourage me to stand and fearlessly cope
Challenges are just every opportunity to show
Either win to earn experience or learn to grow
Your heart and brain jointly speak truly is avow
Leading nature cuts difficulty as aircraft plow
I wish to express my heart to that Angel and say
You become a part of me in every possible way
Being different than other makes you exactly fay
I am optimistic to compensate your debt by pay
At the end, Your presence is a gift of almighty in my life
I am sure we together can make world where love rife

4. My Love Life

A beauty in specs make me feel huge respect,
Our likeness directly intersect still she is perfect;
Her words are sometime stings and sharper than knife,
However, she is my life and wants her to be my wife;
She is not my girlfriend but more than every friend,
We sometime fight but with every fight strengthen our bond;
She keeps herself calm but her eyes speak all,
She neither text me nor she makes any call;
Still with her happiness, I am happy with my love life.
Though we experience happier and bitter moment together,
Her innocent kind heart and soft voice bring me closer;
We are connected to each other with from earlier days,
She entered in my life as my fortune of success rays;
She every-time pretend to be rude, hard and open nature,
Her smiles with glass and esteem manner are my treasure;
She is an intelligent beauty with brain but never express,
Born in modern era still reflect her beauty in traditional dress;
Still with her happiness, I am happy with my love life.

5. Happy Women's Day

I can see the beauty of woman from her eye,
She is understanding, caring, lovely and shy;
The doorway to heart is through her eyes,
Her heart is filled with kindness where only love resides.
Though she faces problem at every step but still give a smile,
She dedicates herself selflessly to protect and takes her family mile;
She could feel the pain of her beloved who is far away without mobile,
Trust me her anger with one whom she loves is temporary and volatile.
A woman plays various role throughout her life,
She may be a mother, sister, daughter or wife;
A beautiful soul lives for happiness of other in life,
She has ability to quickly end all the fight and strife.
My mother is woman who live for me ever,
My sister is a woman who care for me forever;
My lady friends are supportive and perfect bond we share,
I can say frankly that they can never go against me without fear.
I feel every woman should hold same dignity and respect,
I promise to keep up their independence and self-respect;
Everyone must salute her for her sacrifices by all aspect,

Women in the world deserve freedom and equality by immediate effect.
Then we can truly and proudly open our heart to say,
Wishing women's HAPPY WOMEN'S DAY.

VALENTINE WEEK SPECIAL

6. Happy Rose Day

The rose is the symbol of love that heart can know,
The message of love is as clear as white snow.
You are precious like fresh roses that we gather,
I treasure every moment that we spent together.
I look forward to a great future with you ever,
Life will be rainbow of happiness if you are mine forever.
Your beauty is like the rare white rose in the garden grows,
It spread the sweet perfume in the atmosphere it flows.
The perfect roses are richly colored with red,
Love slowly drift into the body, heart and head.
A bud will become rose by slowly being unfold,
We are at stage where our love story can be told.
Roses are beautiful but survive after the thrones all around,
Perfection is handling relation with maturity in the best way is found.
Lastly, rose are a medium to express love and offer to say,
My dear love, wishing you happy rose day.

7. Happy Propose Day

You are smiles of my lips and happiness of my life,
You are the person whom I need as my future wife;
Affection assembles the enjoyment and separate tragic,
You make my day with love in your heart having such magic;
My love bloomed and started floating in the atmosphere,
Thanking you for continuous love, support , share and care;
I request you to Come and live in my heart I won't charge you,
I promise to hold you till death and shall ever support your view;
Your presence with me will ever make a special memorable gather,
It must be joy, fun, lots of love and a special moment being together;
May I request you to kindly share your feeling grow old with me,
We shall get lost in ourselves in the world of happiness vast as sea;
I assure you that will never let tear roll down from your eye,
You have stolen my heart, my consciousness being complete shy;
I promise to protect your self-respect, identity and emotion ever,
I cannot betray you or play with your trust and will happen never;
I assure you will ever be honest, supportive, loving, caring and loyal,

With you holding my hand tightly definitely life would become royal;
It's a request to you Please be the part of me in each and every way,
Dear sweetheart, with lots of love wishing you happy propose day.

8. Happy Chocolate Day

You are my life and sweeter than toffee,
I wish to take you on date for having coffee;
These days chocolates are found of different flavor,
You are beauty with brain who is wise and clever;
I can feel you sugary than Cadbury silk,
You define beauty being as clear as milk;
Snickers and dairy milk bubbly are soft,
I need you as my partner for life at any cost;
Kitkat and choco-bar are rigid and bit tough,
Thanks for being with me either I am smooth or rough;
We both love chocolates of various taste ever,
I need you to live happily in my life forever;
Medicinal candies are rich in ginger, mints and honey,
Your company can never be compensated by money;
Be sweetest of all as chocolate bar every day,
Wishing my dear love happy chocolate day.

9. Happy Teddy Day

There is no one who can take care of me,
I deeply wish to make I and you as we.
I haven't seen any girl who is better than you,
I am really impressed by your simplicity and view.
You are the one with whom I can laugh and cry,
Life without you will be desert and completely dry.
There is no one who can replace and take your place,
Your presence in my life makes me feel being blessed.
There is no one as soft cuddly teddy to show,
I will always hold your hand, you should know.
You are someone who express love in unique way,
My dear love, Wishing you happy teddy day.

10. Happy Promise Day

When you are alone, I will become your shadow;
When you want to cry, I will serve my shoulder;
When you feel sad, I will become your smile;
When you need me, I will become part of you.
When you are low, I will become your endow;
When you want to write, I will become your pen,
When you feel tired to walk, I will become your hypermile;
When you need to speak, I will become your view and voice.
When you are in desert, I will become your meadow;
When you feel shy, I will become love that your heart to pile;
When you want to double, I will become your hand holder;
When you have something to share, I will become ever available.
When you get stuck, I will become your instant path finder;
When you are angry, I will become your cooler & mood swinger;
When you need someone, I will become one among very few;
When you need special care, I will be always there for you.
Trust me, I will become the best part of you in all;
I promise, I will escort you to success being available on a call;
I promise to become your support for life and respect everyday;
Lastly, wishing you happy promise day.

11. Happy Hug Day

Promise is assurity of true relation,
Feeling comes from heart of inner creation.
A hug is representation of my huge love,
Person like you is innocent as dove.
A tight hug can indicate say I missed you,
Person like you is born here very few.
A hug can comfort a crying mind,
Person like you is difficult to find.
A hug can calm you from fear with very ease,
Being is arm of love can cause stress to decrease.
A simple hug can speak all without word,
Your presence is the greatest gift of lord.
A hug can shorten distance between us,
Love grows stronger with a hug just.
A hug can end fight and bring two souls together,
In your absence my heartbeat and breathe gets gather.
A hug can develop trust and joy,
I promise to be a good boy.
A tight hug even though I am far away,
My dear love Wishing you happy hug day.

12. Happy Kiss Day

When two lips meet love gets complete,
Feeling arise and heart start to beat.
Kissing brings two loving souls close,
Symbol of love are heart and red rose.
Kisses are the messenger of love and care,
Simply strengthen the bond that we share.
A heart-tracing kiss decreases all the pain,
Lips together increase happiness as gain.
A kiss burn calories making you fit,
Skip your gym getting relax and seat.
Kissing partner by holding hand can lower stress,
A kiss at morning and bedtime keeps you fresh.
Kiss can bring hearts connect together,
Love cannot find fault with each other.
When words irritate then just pass a kiss,
Our togetherness is what I mostly miss.
One kiss one forehead is sweet gesture by all aspect,
Eliminate lust but full of love and huge respect.
Sending you a kiss though I am far away,
Dear love wishing you happy kiss day.

13. Happy Valentine Day

The wait is over and valentine day is here my love,
Angels are melodiously singing from the heaven above.
There is no one with whom I can ask for love and help,
I am confident being together and mature myself.
I am such a lonely that no one is there for me to scream,
I need you even to keep my hope alive and share my dream.
I can assure there is no one the way you smile and look,
I am just a body living with the heart that you took.
There is no one other than you who can touch my life,
I need you for my breathe, just be my dear wife.
I wish to seal your lips and forever it would stay,
My dear love wishing you Happy Valentine's Day.

BIRTHDAY SPECIAL

14. Happy Birthday

Birthday comes every year but your is special
I am impressed by seeing you kind and social
For any healthy relation loyalty and trust is crucial
Even thinking of live without you makes me glacial
Your bonding of friendship is what almighty gift
Our trust will never decrease to uplift any rift
Promise you it will neither weaken nor ever shift
Understanding and openness will gradually swift
Our relation cannot be stolen or taken away
It will leave message of love and care as spray
keep smiling and keep rocking ever what I always pray
Be happy with joy and wishing you happy birthday

15. Best Wishes to You

Your birthday comes once in a year,
Brings love, smiles and lots to cheer;
Hope you enjoy your memory of past,
There is still fun and success left vast;
Every year you become mature in view,
Today, Wishing happy birthday to you;
Always shine like a star during night,
Enlight darkness and make world bright;
For you, there are all who love and care,
There a lot in your life that you can share;
No one is perfect in life except very few,
Among them wishing happy birthday to you;
A legendary person has born on this day,
Making the universe great place by your way;
we thank god and you for making your presence,
Enjoy the life with full enjoyment and great sense;
Always keep smiling and have success in what you do,
Finally wishes are pouring with happy birthday to you.

16. Happy Birthday Sweetheart

You are my present and want you to be my future,
Undoubtly you are one and only lovable creature;
I have opened my heart after knowing you well,
It's you who is there only in my heart safely dwell;
Moment spend with is ever felt like golden magic,
Surely your birthday celebration is going to be exotic;
No one can care and make you smile the way I do,
Imagine of Life without you is low, sad, dark and blue;
Your teary eye takes me to the dream world of known,
Being blind in your love makes me ever accident prone;
I promise to love you even if my world torn apart,
You are the perfect one who deeply touch my heart;
Today on your birthday I cannot thank god enough,
Giving you as Gift of love to me being kind and tough;
God gave you to me like heavenly present from above,
Wishing you happy birthday to my sweetheart & love.

17. Happy Birthday my Love

Happy birthday to a girl far away in mile,
Who is the reason behind my laughter and smile.
You are precious to me than diamond and gold,
Love for you can never be expressed or told.
Your presence has made my life worthwhile,
Memories shared with you are collected in huge pile.
Heaven is jealous of our love every day and night,
Blessing of God is what connect two hear much tight.
I know you have been there through my tear and fear,
I promise to take this relation for many years.
You have been blessing in my life from up above,
Thanks for being best part of me my dear love.
Meeting you was the best thing ever happened to me,
I wish atleast for once in lifetime we can meet and see.
You are the real beauty princess of the king,
I am sorry I couldn't offer you the love ring.
You are the one whom I see in my every dream,
Thank you for being medicine of my pain and healing cream.
I pray the God to fulfill all desires of your heart,
Promise to always stand with you in any part.

Keep smiling ever and share your view,
Lastly Wishing Happy Birthday to you.

BLEEDING HEART

18. With Broken Heart

My love is not what words can express
My efforts are in vain for you to impress
You leave me alone with no way left to choose
Missing you in life there's nothing else to loose
Sorry for being worst memory for you
I wasn't able to make clear my view
Your smile and happiness what I need
My caring even cannot grow love seed
I have faith & trust in you more than in lord
You entered in my heart being best among shord
Your dream and ambition are much high to fly
Truth is I stand nowhere in your world of sky
Those years of togetherness are best memory for me
Misunderstanding and avoiding can never makes us we
Tussle must not malignant our relation of purity
We lack tolerance & calmness in the sea of maturity
I hold no comparison, you are shining star of knowledge
I never scored those what you made possible in college
You have hands to help and me all alone in life
I must not dare to make you my partner or wife
Don't worry hearts are meant to bleed
Coward like me who got it not to fled

Hope you can successfully chase your dream
Always keep smiling and Shall never scream
Though in rest of life I will miss you ever
You will remain in my heart forever

19. Life without you

I loved you unconditionally and made all effort,
Still our relationship remains a bit short.
We cannot hold on to our love much longer,
But this break has made me much stronger.
Trust me You still hold a special place in my heart,
You were my priority but everything had fallen apart.
I have learnt to hide my pain behind fake painted smile,
To overcome your thought, I keep myself busy with file.
No one can see my pain as I have hidden it for your respect,
But it hurts a lot and my heart keep bleeding I must accept.
I have trust over the God and he will take care of everything,
Nothing is expected and the God who make the final call.
It might we that we weren't meant to be together in this life,
That's why god separated us & you didn't become my wife.
Listen, the fact is that I still love you and can't live without you,
Life has changed a lot but still I feel I am nothing without you.
You are the one for me whom I will keep loving ever,
Trust me, I miss you and will keep missing you forever.
Still if ever, you need my help, just make a call to me,
I promise you that I will always be there for you.

20. HOW CAN I FORGET YOU

My morning begin with you,
My day ends with you,
My nights are made for you,
Then say how can I forget you.

Every sunshine increases hope to meet you,
The Rays of mid-day search the shadow of you,
Evening dim it's light being havoc for you,
Then say how can I forget you..

When I am a body it's heart is you,
When I am a lung it's breath is you,
When I am brain its remote sense is you,
Then say how can I forget you...

Every closing of eyelids brings dream of you,
Every broken piece of me find impression of you,
Every air passing touching me brings feels of you,
Then say how can I forget you....

For this life my future wife is you,
For Ever greenness of my life it's view is you,
For decorative world of happiness its need is you,
Then say how can I forget you.....

In my loneliness there comes memory of you,
My heartbeat shall stop by end of relation with you,
For successful stories of me it's motivation is you,
Then say how can I forget you......

21. My Dear Love, I miss you

My day begin with you and ends with you;
When I close my eye there comes you;
But when I open my eyes, I miss you.
I feel that a big piece of my heart travel with you;
Wherever you go, my heart beats for you;
Every beat says how much I miss you.
I may not be there at present with you;
Calling or chatting is impossible with you;
But trust me, I start to think of you and I miss you.
I am nothing except empty vessel without you;
My smiles and happiness are because of you;
With every distance between us, I miss you.
I am blessed for my life being linked to you;
I keep myself busy with things to do for you;
With passes of every moment, I miss you.
I know staying away is not easy for you;
Don't worry I understand it and I am with you;
But remember my love, I deeply miss you.

Tips To Remain Happy

- We don't meet people by accident. Everyone is meant to cross our path for a reason.
- No one sees what you have done for them but they just see what you don't do.
- Nowadays, people change at exact time when you start considering them your foever.
- love is really powerful because it can make you do things that you would never imagine doing otherwise. That's possible only in love.
- Remember everyone in this earth has a story related to dream, friendship, love, success, failure, struggle, hope, a journey of life or death. it's not necessary every story end with happy ending, some left a lesson behind as well.
- Always give your 100% and be loyal to whatever you do because the truth is in the end of the day, we regret for the choice we didn't make, the love that we didn't accept and the dream we didnt fight for.
- Do remember that you are unique in yourself and when you are correct from yourside then one day someone will definitely hold your hand forever and will be honest, loyal, loving and caring. So, don't give up, keep trying to search right person who is waiting for you as well.

- Never waste your feeling on people who don't care your emotion.
- Love isn't always perfect. It isn't a fairytale or a storybook. And it doesn't always come easy. Love is overcoming obstacles, facing challenges, fighting to be together, holding on & never letting go. It is a short word, easy to spell, difficult to define, & impossible to live without. Love is work, but most of all, Love is realizing that every hour, every minute, & every second was worth it because you did it together.
- Learn from the sun, moon or stars that teaches us a great lesson. It perfectly alright to disappear when things are not at right place but its important is to come back and light brighter again. Same haapen with leaves of tree that shed down in unfavourable weather condition but re-grow again and spread its greenery.

Printed by Libri Plureos GmbH in Hamburg,
Germany